Dirk Nowitzki

Revised Edition

By Jeffrey Zuehlke

AMAZING ATHLETES

L Lerner Publications Company • Minneapolis

For Graham, Tall Teuton

Lerner Publications Company
A division of Lerner Publishing Group, Inc.
241 First Avenue North
Minneapolis, MN 55401 U.S.A.

Website address: www.lernerbooks.com

Library of Congress Cataloging-in-Publication Data

Zuehlke, Jeffrey, 1968–
    Dirk Nowitzki / by Jeffrey Zuehlke. — Rev. ed.
       p.   cm. — (Amazing athletes)
    Includes index.
    ISBN 978-0-7613-9005-3 (pbk. : alk. paper)
    1. Nowitzki, Dirk, 1978-—Juvenile literature. 2. Basketball players—United States—Biography—Juvenile literature. I. Title.
    GV884.N69 Z84 2012
    796.323092—dc23 [B]   2011026211

Manufactured in the United States of America
1 – BP – 12/31/11

TABLE OF CONTENTS

AmericanAirlines Arena was full of fans rooting for the home team, the Miami Heat.

WORLD CHAMPIONS

The huge crowd at AmericanAirlines Arena in Miami, Florida, was nervous. The Dallas Mavericks were beating the Miami Heat by two points in Game Six of the 2011 **National Basketball Association (NBA) Finals**. Dallas had already won three games in the series. If they could win one more, they would be NBA champions!

Dallas **forward** Dirk Nowitzki had only made one basket in the first half. He started the second half with an open shot. *Swish!* But Miami stars LeBron James and Dwyane Wade fought back. This game was going to be close.

The series had been tight so far. The Heat and the Mavericks were evenly matched. But Dirk and his teammates didn't give up.

Dirk passes to a teammate.

A Miami player tries to block Dirk's shot.

Dirk made a tough shot. James answered with a spin and a **layup**. Then Wade made a layup too. Maybe Miami would take the lead. Could Dallas stay ahead?

Not if Dirk and teammate Jason Terry could help it! Terry hit a long **jump shot**. Dirk made another shot as he fell away from the basket. He smiled as the Mavericks took a 10-point lead.

James and Wade did all they could. Time after time in the second half, they charged down the court and tried to score. But Dirk and the Mavs were too strong. As time ran down, James and Wade tried to shoot **three-point baskets**. They needed to score a lot of points quickly to come from behind.

Dirk jumps for the ball.

Dirk knew that his team had to keep scoring to win the game. If Dallas kept making baskets, Miami wouldn't have enough time to catch up. Dirk and his teammates made more shots. Then Dirk made a tough running layup with only a few seconds left in the game. He ran to the other end of the court with his fist in the air. Dirk knew that Dallas had won the game. The final score was Dallas 105, Miami 95. The Mavs were NBA champions!

With less than a minute on the clock, Dirk can finally celebrate.

Dirk ran straight off the court as soon as the game ended. He was so happy that he was crying. He didn't want anyone to see his tears. When he came back to the court, Dirk picked up the NBA championship trophy that he had wanted so badly. He held it high. Finally, Dirk was able to say, "We're world champions."

Dirk holds the NBA championship trophy after winning the NBA Finals. He was also named the championship's Most Valuable Player (MVP).

Wurzburg, where Dirk was born, is located near the center of Germany.

LATE STARTER

Dirk Werner Nowitzki was born June 19, 1978, in Wurzburg, Germany. He comes from a family of talented athletes. Dirk's father, Joerg, plays and coaches a game called team handball. Dirk's mother, Helga, played basketball on the German national team. Even Dirk's older sister, Silke, is a talented basketball player.

Soccer is the most popular sport in Germany. Dirk grew up playing soccer and team handball. "I didn't start basketball until I was 12 or 13," Dirk says. But once he tried out the game, he found he was very good at it.

By the time he was 16, Dirk was playing for his hometown's professional team, the Wurzburg X-Rays. His skills caught the attention of a local basketball coach, Holger Geschwindner. The coach saw that Dirk had the talent to be a great player. But he knew that Dirk had a lot to learn.

As a youngster, Dirk wasn't interested in doing his schoolwork. But Coach Geschwindner told him that he had to practice with his mind as well as his body. "If you want to be a good player," he told Dirk, "you have to learn how to learn."

Geschwindner offered to coach Dirk. "I can make your son the best player in Germany," he told Dirk's parents. "And he can play in the NBA if he will commit to working with me."

The Nowitzkis agreed. Dirk was eager to learn. He and his coach spent hours and hours practicing. "Without [Geschwindner], I wouldn't be where I am," says Dirk. "He taught me how to shoot, how to move, how to play. I owe him everything. He is like a second dad."

Dirk's play kept getting better. He perfected his shooting.

Holger Geschwindner taught Dirk many of the basketball skills that he uses in the NBA.

He worked hard on his rebounding. In March 1998, he and several other European players were invited to show off their talent in the United States. Nineteen-year-old Dirk flew to San Antonio, Texas, to play in the Nike Hoops Summit game. He and his teammates played against a team of top American high school players.

Each year, talented young basketball players from around the world play in the Nike Hoops Summit.

Dirk was the star of the game. He scored 33 points and grabbed 14 rebounds. He also made 19 of 23 free throws.

Dirk's incredible play caught the attention of many NBA teams. He decided to try his luck in the upcoming NBA **draft**. A few months later, Dirk was chosen in the first round by the Milwaukee Bucks. The Bucks traded him to the Dallas Mavericks.

Steve Nash (right) was already a star when Dirk joined the Mavs.

TAKING OFF

Dirk accepted the challenge of playing in the NBA. He joined a Dallas team that already had two great players—**guards** Steve Nash and Michael Finley. Would Dirk be good enough to play alongside them?

After a bad game, Dirk works extra hard to improve. "He has a key to the gym, and if he has a bad game, he comes back that night to shoot," says Mavs owner Mark Cuban.

Dirk struggled at first. NBA players were much bigger, stronger, and faster than the players he had faced in Germany. At seven feet, Dirk was one of the league's tallest players. But he was very skinny. The big NBA players could push him around easily.

But Dirk's teammates supported him. "He was so down on himself," says Nash. "There were a lot of times when I would have to pump him up." Dirk and Nash spent hours working on their skills together. The two became best friends.

By his second season, Dirk was starting to catch on. He put up strong scoring and

rebounding numbers. He averaged more than 17 points and 6 rebounds per game. He finished second in the voting for the NBA's Most Improved Player award.

As Dirk started to play well in the NBA, he became more popular with fans.

Dirk, Nash, and Finley were making the high-scoring Mavs an exciting team to watch. The 2000–2001 season was a great year for Dirk and his team. Dirk averaged nearly 22 points and just over 9 rebounds per game. He was named to the **All-NBA Team**.

The Mavs won 53 games and made it to the **playoffs** for the first time in years. They defeated the Utah Jazz in an exciting first-round series. But they lost to the San Antonio Spurs in the Western **Conference** Semifinals.

Dirk puts up a shot against Utah in the first round of the 2000–2001 playoffs.

BETTER AND BETTER

The Mavs knew that Dirk was their star of the future. Before the 2001–2002 season, they signed him to a huge **contract**. Dirk agreed to play for the Mavs for the next six seasons. The Mavs would pay him $79 million!

Dirk earned his big money with fantastic play. He averaged more than 23 points a game. He was also selected to play in his first NBA All-Star Game.

Steve Nash praised his teammate and best friend. "[Dirk's] always getting better," he said. "When he arrived in Dallas, we didn't know if he could play with us. Now we ask ourselves if we're good enough to play with him."

Steve Nash *(left)*, Dirk *(center)*, and Michael Finley *(right)* made the Mavs an exciting team to watch.

Dirk and Nash powered the Mavs to another great season. The team won 57 games and made it to the semifinals again. But they could not get past the Spurs.

Dirk's fifth season was his best yet. In 2002–2003, he upped his scoring average to more than 25 points a game. He was again named to the NBA All-Star Game. Dirk, Nash, and Finley were the team's leaders and best players. They earned the nickname the Big Three.

The Mavs won a whopping 60 games during the 2002–2003 season. In the playoffs, they blasted their way to the conference finals. Dirk's team lost to the Spurs in six games.

Losing to the Spurs was tough. But the 2003–2004 season was even tougher.

Dirk loves music. He can often be found listening to his iPod. One of Dirk's favorite hobbies is playing the saxophone.

Although the Mavs won 52 games, they lost in the first round of the playoffs.

Sadly, the Big Three would never get a chance to win it all. Before the 2004–2005 season, Steve Nash signed a contract to play for the Phoenix Suns. The Big Three was no more.

Dirk was upset that the Mavs had let his best friend leave. He knew he would have to play even better to keep Dallas near the top. Dirk was ready for the challenge.

Dirk missed Nash after he left the team in 2004.

Dallas fans gather around a seven-foot-tall statue of Dirk made of Legos.

ONE OF THE BEST

The Mavs won 58 games in the 2004–2005 season. But once again, Dirk and his teammates couldn't get it done in the playoffs. They lost to the Phoenix Suns in the second round.

Dirk takes most of his shots from far away, but he has learned to score close to the basket as well.

In 2005–2006, Dirk finally beat Nash and the Phoenix Suns in the conference finals. Dirk and the Mavs then moved on to face the Heat in the NBA Finals. The Heat beat the Mavs in six games.

The next season was great for Dirk. He was named the NBA's MVP. But Dallas still lost early in the playoffs.

For the next three seasons, the Mavs made it to the playoffs only to be beaten in the early rounds. But Dirk wasn't going to give up. He knew that he could bring a championship to Dallas.

Dirk chose to play for Germany in the 2008 Summer Olympics in Beijing, China. Dirk carried the German flag in the opening ceremony. This is a big honor for an athlete.

Dirk dribbles past an opponent during a 2008 Olympic game.

Dirk finally got his championship in 2010–2011. The entire basketball world seemed to be cheering for Dirk and his Mavs to beat the Heat. Dirk was named Best Male Athlete and Best NBA Player at the 2011 ESPYs, an awards show for athletes. He threw out the first pitch at a Texas Rangers baseball game. But Dirk's favorite gift came from Muhammad Ali, the famous boxer. Ali gave Dirk a boxing glove on which he had written, "You are the Greatest."

Dirk poses with one of his awards at the 2011 ESPYs.

Thanks to a lot of hard work, Dirk made himself one of the best basketball players in the world. When someone asked him how it felt to be a champion, Dirk said, "I still really can't believe it. We worked so hard and so long for it."

Dirk takes a shot against the Los Angeles Lakers during a game in which he scored his 20,000th point. Dirk was the first player from Europe to score 20,000 points in the NBA.

After winning the NBA championship, Dirk's teammates joked that he could finally take a day off. But he won't relax for long. "Every season, I want some part of my game to be better than it was the year before," Dirk says.

Dirk gets ready to throw the first pitch at a Texas Rangers baseball game in 2011. Instead of a baseball, Dirk threw a basketball.

Selected Career Highlights

2010–2011   Named NBA Finals Most Valuable Player
Named to Western Conference All-Star team for the tenth time

2009–2010   Became the first European-born player to score at least 20,000 points in the NBA
Named to Western Conference All-Star team for the ninth time

2008–2009   Named to Western Conference All-Star team for the eighth time

2007–2008   Became Mavs' all-time leading scorer
Named to Western Conference All-Star team for the seventh time
Played for Germany in the Summer Olympics

2006–2007   Named NBA Most Valuable Player
Named to Western Conference All-Star team for the sixth time

2005–2006   Named to the Western Conference All-Star team for the fifth time
Finished third in voting for NBA Most Valuable Player
Led Mavericks to the NBA Finals for the first time
Scored a season-high 51 points against the Golden State Warriors

2004–2005   Named to the Western Conference All-Star team for the fourth time
Scored a career-high 53 points in a game against the Houston Rockets

2003–2004   Led the Mavericks in scoring average with 21.8 points per game
Led the Mavericks in rebounds per game with 8.7
Named to the Western Conference All-Star team for the third time
Made a career-high 8 three-point baskets in a game against the Seattle Supersonics

2002–2003   Led the Mavericks in scoring average with 25.1 points per game
Led the Mavericks in rebounds per game with 9.9
Mavericks leading scorer in 50 games
Named to the Western Conference All-Star team for the second time

2001–2002	Grabbed a career-high 23 rebounds in a game against the Boston Celtics
	Led the Mavericks in scoring average with 23.4 points per game
	Led the Mavericks in rebounds per game with 9.9
	Mavericks leading scorer in 40 games
	Mavericks leading rebounder in 44 games
	Named to the Western Conference All-Star team for the first time
2000–2001	Named to All-NBA team for the first time
	Led the Mavericks in scoring average with 21.8 points per game
	Led the Mavericks in rebounds per game with 9.2
	Scored 10 or more points in 80 games
1999–2000	Finished second in voting for NBA's Most Improved Player
	Averaged 17.5 points and 6.5 rebounds per game
1998–1999	Averaged 8.2 points and 3.4 rebounds per game
	Scored a season-high 29 points in a game against the Phoenix Suns

Glossary

All-NBA Team: a team of the best 15 players in the NBA. The All-NBA Team is chosen at the end of each NBA season.

conference: one of two groups of teams in the NBA. The groups are the Western Conference and the Eastern Conference. The winner of the Western Conference Finals meets the winner of the Eastern Conference Finals in the NBA Finals.

contract: a written deal signed by a player and a team. The player agrees to play for a team for a stated number of years. The team agrees to pay the player a stated amount of money.

draft: a yearly event in which professional teams in a sport are given the chance to pick new players from a selected group

forward: a player on a basketball team who usually plays close to the basket. Forwards need to rebound and shoot the ball well.

guard: a player on a basketball team whose main job is to handle the ball. Guards need to be good passers and shooters.

jump shot: a play in which the player jumps and shoots the ball at a distance from the basket

layup: a shot attempted from close range

National Basketball Association (NBA) Finals: the NBA's championship series. The team that wins four games in the series becomes the NBA champion.

playoffs: a series of contests played after the regular season has ended. Teams compete to become the champion.

rebounding: grabbing the ball after a missed shot

three-point baskets: a long-range shot that counts for three points

Further Reading & Websites

Kennedy, Mike, and Mark Stewart. *Swish: The Quest for Basketball's Perfect Shot*. Minneapolis: Millbrook Press, 2009.

Savage, Jeff. *Dwyane Wade*. Minneapolis: Lerner Publications Company, 2007.

Savage, Jeff. *LeBron James*. Minneapolis: Lerner Publications Company, 2012.

Savage, Jeff. *Steve Nash*. Minneapolis: Lerner Publications Company, 2007.

Dirk Nowitzki Fan Site
http://www.41fan.net/en/index.html
Find out the latest news about Dirk's life and career from his official fan site.

Espn.com
http://espn.com
Espn.com covers all the major professional sports, including NBA basketball.

Official Site of the Dallas Mavericks
http://www.nba.com/mavericks
Find out the latest Mavs news from the team's official site.

Sports Illustrated Kids
http://www.sikids.com
The *Sports Illustrated Kids* website covers all sports, including basketball.

Index

Photo Acknowledgments

The images in this book are used with the permission of: © Chris Chambers/ Getty Images, p. 4; REUTERS/Hans Deryk, p. 5; AP Photo/Tom DiPace, p. 6; © Ronald Martinez/Getty Images, p. 7; © Michael Laughlin/Sun-Sentinel/ ZUMA Press, p. 8; AP Photo/David J. Phillip, p. 9; © Witold Skrypczak/ SuperStock, p. 10; © Michael Mulvey/Dallas Morning News/CORBIS, p. 12; © Andy Lyons/Allsport/Getty Images, p. 13; AP Photo/Kent Horner, p. 15; AP Photo/Joerg Sarbach, p. 17; © George Frey/AFP/Getty Images, p. 18; AP Photo/Diether Endlicher, p. 19; AP Photo/Elaine Thompson, p. 20; © Jose Luis Villegas/Sacramento Bee/ZUMA Press, p. 22; © Charlie Neuman/The San Diego Union-Tribune/ZUMA Press, p. 23; © Hector Amezcua/Sacramento Bee/ZUMA Press, p. 24; REUTERS/Lucy Nicholson, p. 25; © Kevin Mazur/WireImage/Getty Images, p. 26; AP Photo/Tony Gutierrez, p. 27; © Jim Cowsert/US Presswire, p. 28; © Erich Schlegel/CORBIS, p. 29.

Front cover: AP Photo/Lynne Sladky.

Main body text set in PMN Caecilia 16/28. Typeface provided by Linotype AG.